THE MAN ON THE WATER

W. S. Di Piero

a plume editions book

AN IMPRINT OF MADHAT PRESS

ASHEVILLE, NORTH CAROLINA

MadHat Press
MadHat Incorporated
PO Box 8364, Asheville, NC 28814

The Library of Congress has assigned
this edition a Control Number of
2016920080

ISBN 978-1-941196-40-3 (paperback)

Cover art and design by Marc Vincenz
Book design by MadHat Press
Author portrait by Paul Resika

www.MadHat-Press.com

First Printing

Also by W. S. Di Piero

Poetry

The First Hour
The Only Dangerous Thing
Early Light
The Dog Star
The Restorers
Shadows Burning
Skirts and Slacks
Brother Fire
Chinese Apples: New and Selected Poems
Nitro Nights
TOMBO

Essays

Memory and Enthusiasm: Essays 1975–1985
Out of Eden: Essays on Modern Art
Shooting the Works: On Poetry and Pictures
City Dog
When Can I See You Again: New Art Writings

Translations

Pensieri, by Giacomo Leopardi
This Strange Joy: Selected Poems of Sandro Penna
The Ellipse: Selected Poems of Leonardo Sinisgalli
Ion, Euripides

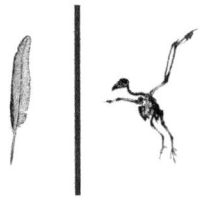

TABLE OF CONTENTS

THE MAN ON THE WATER

The Words

When they were young, tender-tough, exposed,
desiring experience but not knowing they desired,
words lived in small dense neighborhoods as sounds
without meaning, but street smarts shaped them
into a kind of plainsong that in time cried itself
into language, a pond-scum shape of sentences,
dragonflies, red dragonflies, and toads and reeds,
the longer the sentences, the more the words
wished for and wanted to claim, the more they felt
like stuff, like honeycomb and hair combs,
billy clubs, skinks, cardboard, silks, and concrete,
and soon became the things they said they were,
they imagined living other lives as other things,
like red rivets on bridge towers and the photons
glinting there, or crushed oyster shells and the drive
they cover in some bayou parish, in time the words
became one mind that owned it all, that lived
as if it could be alive with all things all at once,
a dreamed-up city crying sweet throaty noise,
but soon they became low-down, slutty with desire,
derelict, living off the streets, begging small change,
attaching themselves there, here, and our words,
just like that, become us, they are what we have
and yet still want so badly that it hurts.

Wheels, Fenders, Windshields, Hoods

It tasted bitter, burnt, like most things that summer,
the medicinal orange-peel darkness in the shot glass,
the day's damp heavy veils forming around the sun,
around groggy lumps in work-boots opening car doors,
while she, at 5 a.m., in her silence and widowed blacks
sat across from me and my young, stupid years.
Her mottled hands showed me what was what:
a Fernet shot, butter brimming the toast,
raw eggs I sucked from rococo old-country cups,
biscotti to dunk in bitter coffee—they'd bear me
like the man I might become, through the dark
to work the line at Ford's Pennsauken Depot.
I hardly knew her, my grandmother's sister,
but took her tomato-and-mayo sandwiches
on hot close rides with men in white T-shirts
who rolled the windows down and smoked or snored.
Lunchtime, lying inside shipping crates we built
along the line, picking and loading stock, I read
our defective Catholics, *Dubliners, Brighton Rock*,
their sentences like foreign languages or chants
or calls. And magnanimous Whitman, Durrell
and his olive trees, and beautiful broken Delmore,
how I loved him, he was educated, he could sing—
Time is the fire in which we burn. I was myself
a squealing snotnose rhapsody, reading on breaks:

I wanted out, a world elsewhere, no more dialects
and hoagies, alley fights and fake florals,
women's voices ripping space to rags,
pasty summers, packing grease, and Tastykakes.
After work, back from Jersey, the light softened
South Philly's brick and glass. Paul Klee said to me:
a drawing is taking a line for a walk, so take it
for a walk that becomes a sentence in lines.
Neighbors on front steps, transistors, the pretzel guy
banging his bell, and Good Humor's pathetic tinkle.
No music or TV inside her house of shades.
I spent those summer hours, one year short
of getting out, finally, reading for my life
in her son's room. She didn't talk about it,
the secret they all observed: curtains drawn,
she sat and crocheted the Sacred Heart,
while Nico, Angelo, Tino, whatever his name was,
abided absent from her parlor: while upstairs
I heeded voices, the long-gone son chain-smoked,
serving time, doing eternal push-ups
in Eastern State Penitentiary, a murder charge,
who he killed I never knew. She sat heavily
in the burnt-almond dark of her house undelivered
from all that, the misbegotten, the unforgiven,
time embittered by time. That summer before I left

3

the village life that reared me and put ashes
in my mouth and anger in my stifled wild heart,
I lodged in his room, ate raw eggs, got angrier,
hungrier for words in smart disturbing orders:
Zi' Mari' saw me off to work, where we hid crickets,
from the unassembled crates stored outdoors,
inside our foreman's desk, what a prick,
he pushed the line to ace his Christmas bonus,
Shorty Boyle was his name, I curse him forever here,
our crickets made him flap his lips and blubber,
mockery of the water world, uglier than catfish
that filled The Lakes, where only black folks fished.
I can say here the impossible, the silly, the true.
Who's listening? Zi' Mari', when did you die?
Old sorrowful woman, your son is still upstairs,
you hardly spoke a word, I speak back to you now,
and serve you this, my dear, in the near dark.

The Family Circle

1. Somebody Say Grace

Here we are again, Friday night
in that Watkins Street kitchen
with our serious friend, Silence,
and her clenched, unpleasant cousins,
Fault and Grievance. I'm the child,
so they must love me. Pop gets tripe
stewed in red sauce and beer.
The tripe forgives his few brown teeth.
Dad's dazed and grim before his slice
of fried boloney, his boiled beets,
the merry meatballs of last week
a sorry memory now: they'll reconvene
upon the oilcloth some day soon.
What can our Dago family say
on its way to America, to sweet corn
and true chocolate, where the TV set
gasses the house with eager voices?
Nobody talks much in America
at this table, still shipping on its way
to America. Pop cranks his tongue,
Dad starts to cry. But why? Who knows?
And Mom indicts the poor potatoes
she pokes and sticks with an angry fork.

Here it is that we remain, at this board,
uttering aspirations, giving thanks
for what we're not and won't soon be.

2. The Aspirations

They aren't seeking anything. They want.
They don't know what they want.
So here they are as usual, their boy,
devoutly short of breath, on his knees,
dog-face earnest, while across from Dad
mother's ruby nails pinch her rosary
toward pain, and her husband studies
a dark floor that must look far away.
Their boy after supper leads them
around aspirations he's memorized.
He aspires to he knows not what,
Mother of God Have Mercy On Us,
you know what I mean? And also,
for Christ's sake, Sacred Heart of Jesus,
I was saying, save us sinners, now,
Merciful Mother Please Do Us Right.
And is Pop still alive? Dead? We *forgot?*
Hey ho the daffy boy leads them,

but they look weary and already old.
Mom won't let Dad forget it's two days
since he shaved, and has sister disappeared
into a wood? No woods in the neighborhood!
Ah, there she is, the little sister we forgot,
in finger curls and pinafore, who quakes
while the ejaculations purr around
the tight lost circle they compose.

Catch You at the Oregon

Steam finagled your hair, the amber shades clouded
behind the coffee lines you blew across the cup—
you sipped and tuned things out, the world can wait.
That was this time last year. I just fell into it again.
You seemed to be watching us be there, or observing
some other history. The scene had no meaning,
it was an ordinary decorated moment,
the shades, your head, circus-hoop earrings, steam,
but I'd dropped into the cylinder where events toss
with others from other times and make a noise:
one of the restored F-line trolleys sledded past,
Robin Hood green streamlined by a sharp red stripe,
the same one I'm sure I rode in 1956, down 9th Street,
past Horn and Hardart's baloney and lemon meringue:
Eisenhower's pruney face on the morning news,
after jerky images of Budapest, said the United States
shall not intervene: Old World streets, broken bottles,
smoke, rocks, rags, college kids, even girls in skirts,
threw bricks and stood in the path of Russian tanks.
Gangrenous politics never meets our need for sense,
the world's force can't be transformed to grace,
the conviction that the world defeats us rose
like a sickness of unreason in the childish me.
What our innocent diner scene reminded me of,
when that trolley went past, wasn't just Ike's

tweedy black-and-white-TV moment, one more
storm of a moment, any moment in bloody time:
that trolley I was talking about terminated
near the stainless-jacketed Oregon Diner,
its ashtrays, linoleum, hot roast beef sandwiches,
where we boys, years past Budapest, in our useless
sexed-up chaos, finished our famished nights.
I remember mostly not the coffee but the steam,
how it seeped from everything, though I know
that can't be so, from urns, grill, menus, jukebox,
and the high hair of our pudgy waitress, Fran.
By then late night news in living color flashed
different faraway wars and their dead kids.
Where are you now? You with your buggy shades
who never rode an historic trolley car till now
I say it's so. I'm still here across from you.
Weird grainy steam hangs in the air of things.

W. S. Di Piero

Egypt at Pep's

Now still here
as I was then
the somber child
in a car window
observing pigeons
flying sideways
through great buildings
and grand cricket
fire escapes:
and the syph
we ridiculed
hitch-stepping past
Voodoo Lou's
shrunken-head shop
down South Street
near neon Pep's
where Yusef Latiff
wailed mizmar snake-
charming songs:
I still haven't
passed them by,
they didn't pass me,
these all-my-life
laminated sheets
wrapped opaque

around my heart;
the hours didn't go
anywhere but here,
pressing harder by
the day, the days.
Outside Pep's
I'm here down
my newest street:
I tell myself to sing,
sing things austere and vast
as magic-lantern panes.
The ravens mind
the chimneypots,
and over on Fillmore,
where Rasselas folded,
the CD vendor
stands his corner,
though the flugelhorns
trombones vibes
have left the clubs
for concert halls.
Abstraction has
its sheer beauty
but diminishes us,
while a ripe banjoist

somewhere down
some other street
sings "Roxanne."

The Rain So Cold

The air of the day abhors us
and drives outliers like her
inside the crowded train.
She speed-talks *it hurts*
my eyes it's too wet
like wet whatever
and cold in my eyes.
I ride the length of town
with her and smiling nuns,
skateboards, teens kissing,
toddlers on leashes,
Mission Bay to Ocean Beach.
Wet riders come and go.
The orator and I hold firm.
Who gives alms to Poor Tom
when the foul fiend vexes?
The rain lets up:
out on the sidewalks
Asian gleaners appear
with smiley-face latex gloves
and XXL garbage bags,
neatly dressed, picking through
the city's sinuses,
fastidious and focused
among the street singers

13

and their pussy scabs split
across raw fatty hands:
they sing to their doubles,
the elementals and invisibles
whose squeaky vocals reel
from tree roots and concrete.

In the Marina

It squeezes the spleen
this sunny winter's
New Year's morning,
not the pain itself
but the too much of it,
the inexcusable with
its perfect right to exist,
the grass shining bright
along Marina Green,
the tipping masts,
the small tide that raps
piers and rolling hulls
creaking, while you weep
harder into the cold wind:
your hot pain loves this
anniversary of his death
the wind carries through
your loud red blouse,
broken hoarse voice,
and flighty hands
the wind can't calm.
Kiddies wrangle their bikes
through our promenade,
elders, us, dogs, him,
lovers on their elbows

on all this perfumed grass,
so why not cry out for what's
not here and the too much
that walks along with it?

TO SFO

The nude, a naked woman,
materializes in a condo window:
her houselights expand the frame
he now steps into, dressed to go,

like me, at 5:30 a.m., on my way
among the cabs and headlights and reds
in their blasted speedway corridors.
The moonlight spanks the waters.

The come and go of local life fills me
with sadness. Time hurts. Where am I?
(Rte. 101 S, out of San Francisco.) Where
am I going? (Newark, then New York

and its peoples.) The terminal's noise
sirens weird silence. On the Jetway,
we all pretend we're not about to rise
into the heavens that once were there.

Soon I'll be fearless among best-sellers,
jaunty screens, stale feet, cold fries,
gorilla backpacks, Blake's screeching babes
bounced by parents in cargo pants …

Our diverse unrest confers on me
an obliging calm and aggrieved patience.
The nude in the window stays with me,
and the moment of her man, inviolable,

steady in mind, a momentous ordinary,
as I fly between a grape sweatshirt
who tanked in Reno, and she who walked
unhappily from her still-good marriage.

The Man On The Water

December's wind jerks spindrift puppets
down Chicago's River: they flee the water
they're made from, they wade in it, walk on it,

they inflate into hourglass coils that spray
into nothing and collapse while he's rigged,
two streets over, to IVs in the chemo room.

The crocus will pop, the forsythia shake its yellow.
It's hard to think of the sparings of spring.
I've never felt so hurt by hard, blown cold.

The crows, our wise brothers, beat against
the feathered grains that populate the river.
Michigan Ave., late morning, the ironwork bridge:

I should see his diminished form gray and fugitive
upon the water. I don't. The wind blows too hard.
Rude Chicago how beautiful you are your mukluks

parkas mittens mufflers. Hardly anybody's here.
Where did they all go? The cancer's in blood and bone.
The bitterness slows me. The wind licks scratches

on my face not my face. In October he'd been all
bones and scraped skin, four weeks in hospital,
home for Halloween, when the twins kicked up

the tumbling cereal leaves and slapped at them.
An ice-cream cart beeped through charred air.
The trick-or-treaters dragged or swung big bags.

I felt the gentle gusts create more time around us.
A neighbor's spring-loaded pop-up whiskered ghoul
sensed our presence and arose from its stubble yard.

We forget too much. In an hour I'll pick him up.
Next day the girls screamed and cried when we passed
the dormant cobwebbed thing that once greeted us.

Their Winter Songs

The cranes are singing their sad songs across
the Sacramento River's Prospect Slough,
as they flew over Dante's head in hell,
files of carnal souls condemned to live
a million million times their gorgeous sins
of loving lust and corrupted mind, crying
their eternal patterns of useless come and go.
Their whippy files sweep the air: they want
to catch sight of love's body in the Pilgrim
who visits their pain just that one time. What songs
did they not really sing? Engines and tires whish
outside my steamy bus, its tender lovers
chewing sandwiches and pears. Above,
the cranes sing that love is a waving line
in motion, in the wind, composed or deranged,
a passage in passage, a dampened, staggered trill,
as if practicing to find their voice again
and sing more of the lost. They remind me
how love's blood rushes to weary memory.
Dante's souls go nowhere for all time.
We bone-and-tissue creatures stir up embers
of fiery wish, we sing our aggrieved lais
to one another, while the cranes white out
beyond the horizon's stormy, late-day fires.

W. S. Di Piero

Jersey Sheets from Jersey

I watched a sleepy boy on Sunday,
still in his icy blue pajamas,
revolve inside the sudsy washer
with sheets and sleeping bags.
I think his mother left him there.

His face dissolves inside the drum.
He's jellyfish, kelp, manatee, foam.
He must be having fun. He rubs his face
against the glass, this squirmy boy
I was. To live past childhood

was such a dreary effort, outside
the drum, lost as I was to images
draining in my head. I feared the world.
It hurt to live in it unmothered.
The tumbling boy is safe, couched, slow.

*

Hey, lover girl, I tried to clear the sheet's
semen lube sweat pinkish blood and wine
we tasted on pluvial March nights:
amethyst sheets from Hackensack that chafed
before we broke them in. That really was

my marbled face behind the door,
the rinse cycle revenant who won't
give up. Amethyst, your stone, charm
against pain poison mischance loss,
the gem of dreams' gooey flexions.

To sleep in one another's arms,
heedless of loss yet turbulent
with dreams of your blue parakeets
in catacombs, your daddy costumed
in his coffin as the Queen of Hearts.

*

Black boys in my neighborhood,
who never crossed into our streets,
begged house to house, their Halloween
dispensation, in old-man overcoats,
corked faces, and nylon stocking caps.

Did I tell you that? What else to say?
We animals long to be together in
an instant of out-of-time time while in
this rapid riddled here and now.
The ceiling fans will cool us down.

The voices inside the wall must be
that couple arguing. Someone left
big boisterous flowers in the hall.
Why do we feel as if the flowers
are filling up with trembling us?

"What a Fabulous View You Have"

Some houses start to tick alive with lamps.
The hospital's white windows don't flinch.
Parnassus Ave., down below, arches its back:
your finger, in those years, traced its spine
up and down my unwashed windows. The sea
gives off pinky particulate vapors. No sun yet.
The moon's full, Shiva's moon of ways and ends.

You changed the ways. My new habit's yours.
Your mousey hours, pushing 3 a.m.
when you went to bed, were three hours short
of when I used to wake to start my day,
start the work. That old me left home with you.
Your rhythms outlived us: now I'm up late
like you, sleep two hours, then am up again,

like now, before I hit my second sleep:
the radio tower's pulsing red lights plead
unconsoling constancy: one house,
invisible in the woods below, ignites
a cat's cradle of crystal lights that pop
in zany sequences, like happiness
or alarm or something worse. It's October,

I look to find someone like me looking out
and back at me from windows across the way.
The fake snow of rooftops painted white glows
in dull remnant moonlight that also fell
on those air plants you brought to me and to
this garden of a kitchen of work, its fruit, knives, CDs,
unruly pages, dear screen, old address books …

In time, the garden-center lady said, they'll bloom,
but give them tons of direct sunlight.
They bloomed but didn't last. Their fuzzy skin
made you want to pet them. I'm marking time,
saying nothing, really, except I feel
I've assumed your watch, this hour of this world,
and will pay attention to whatever stirs.

The Sidewalk Harvest

They must be moving, maybe changing towns.
Here's the saw he sized their bedstead on,
and flatware, cheerful flattened beach balls,
throw rugs, highball glasses, steamer trunk.
It takes too many weeks to move. See them
punish their small rooms and obese garage
with an unloved silence they've somehow learned
they can't live without: and out from that silence
they gently drop aggrieved, pale, sincere words
into the children's hair, who hardly hear.

He used to balance on this gimpy ladder,
and with these hard-caked gloves rake sodden leaves
from sagging gutters that engorged and poured
shredded sheets of winter rain outside
their ashy windows. She wept in reckless spring
over her chives and holy basil that he
chopped and dropped in restless stews and soups
that simmered in these earnest pans now stacked
like tipsy chapeaus with no party to attend.
Passing cars slow down to view the goods.

Where will they go, the opaline lampshade
and stopped clocks and diamond paste,
while he and she won't anymore be telling

how the day went, who called, what kiddo did.
And don't forget the comforter, those stains
that we deposited like essences.
Remember us then? We thought we were
plummy immigrants so fresh to life
and anything strange. Desirous, too,
though what we desired we could not tell.

Bright strangers to this dimmed imperium
now pull up, ask our best price for blender,
unfinished quilt, broke rocker and broke books
and faulty shelves, the drop-leaf table, the dresser,
and bed-frame parts I planned out and true-cut
as a kit we'd break down then rejoin
whenever we made our next big move
and reclaimed our lives, our unconscious days—
the kit would make it all much simpler when
we lay in one another's arms, told stories, and slept.

Inside "The Last Drop"

Behind says, *Yo, behind!*
Tootie pauses at the pour
and lets him pass behind,
while evening comes down
in the darker fall, still time
for loneliness, but not now.
The ice buckets, tickets, kegs,
the goblet she turns as if
to make it disappear inside
the stupendous handkerchief.
O Tootie, your smile's invincible,
and Doc, in his corner spot,
says growing up back east
on an evening like this,
a 1950s All Souls' Day,
moms called kids indoors
when the furnaces vented:
gray ghosts ran through the air.
But Pittsburgh isn't here,
a big brushed moon rising,
when Tootie's honeybun
swings through the doors,
wearing autumn's sugared light.
A kiss across the bar
and close words I can't hear

intensify our moment—
the peppery desert wind
jiggles the screen door,
the light on honeybun
becomes a pilgrim soul
arrived among us,
and we're gathered here
to greet it, witness it
conferred on his tensile girl.
Stay with us, Tootie, O Rootie,
you and your too-long legs
and squeaky boo-boo voice,
while we transpire here
in delight, with the ghosts
who keep us company.

The Processionals

Jet-lagged and a little drunk after "As Time Goes By" and
    other standards
in a rathskeller fake juke joint in Florence, Christmas Eve,
    1992,
I walked the piazza with other shades sliding across the walls,
the starless sky, the murderous palazzo, the timid Arno close
but quieted: on a stone bench, lovers mismatched in years
    held hands,
making an imperfect painful art of an impossible perfect one.
After dark, strangers and their sea-sound murmurs stir
in and out of lamplight. The postcard kiosk still burns bright.
We're inhaling gristly winter airs: past solstice, I feel slow
and fat with time, new time. Under the small cocky David,
two English bulldogs pull on a leash like monsters dragged
from underground by their lady's rhinestone purse and fox-
    head stole.
Herakles clubs the helpless Caco. Perseus lifts Medusa's
    orgasmic head.
Around such ecstasy of force a beautiful choral laughter rules
the airwaves around our heads. I'm at home in all this
    strangeness.
Hopeless Caco begs for deliverance. Cables drain from
    Medusa's head.
I hear them before I see them: saffron robes over union suits,
flip-flops, woolen socks, the Krishna initiates *chingching*-ing

like the tribe they were, emerging from the narrowest lane
where bulldogs, dame, kiosk, and I and others wait for them:
the bouncy slow procession timed to their finger chimes,
airy voices in happy adoration, unaware subversives
of our scene, a novelty act, a dancing gang of believers:
their shadows, too, walked across the walls in eggnog light,
then drifted down another lane. There and gone, like that,
like us, strangers to places, at home there, the music
a sprint of time, a something joy, a salty aromatic bread.

These Early Fall Days

I don't want wisdom, don't want the one
and every summed in potentate words
that parade on yellow leaves from gums
and ginkgos that shake their trashy skirts
to shiver color to this floor of things.

I don't want we. No choice oinker phrases.
I want the silver safety pin so bright
in that girl's lip, and seasonal silver
to foil the air like silver-leaf oaks
in their flush finalities. No ratiocination.

Butterscotch, lanolin, yes, agrodolce airs,
plasma, ores, recycling-bin realities,
troubled angels in posses on Market Street.

No conclusions from red leaves on grass and sidewalk,
from leaf-bits on my fingers and near noise that stitches
fall's debris falling down the towers of air.

Acknowledgements

"The Words," "Wheels, Fenders, Windshields, Hoods," "Catch You at the Oregon," and "The Processionals" first appeared in *The Threepenny Review*.

"In the Marina" and "The Sidewalk Harvest" in *Kenyon Review*.

"The Family Circle" in *New England Review*.

"'What a Fabulous View You Have'" and "The Rain So Cold" in *Plume Poetry*.

ABOUT THE AUTHOR

SIMONE DI PIERO received the 2012 Ruth Lilly Prize for lifetime achievement. He's the author of many books of poetry, essays, and translations. He has written frequently about the visual arts and contributes a regular column on art to the *San Diego Reader.* He lives in San Francisco.

* 9 7 8 1 9 4 1 1 9 6 4 0 3 *